LOKI'S GAM

B

TANYA WHITE

"I detest what you say, but I will defend to the death your right to say it"

(Voltaire *attrib.*)

"MAGNA EST VERITAS ET PRAEVALET"

(Mighty is the truth and it prevails)

Book of Esdras, Vulgate

For my dear old friends and colleagues, David and Sara., who have worked tirelessly in the pursuit of justice while retaining the greatest gift of all, a free spirit

Biography

Tanya White is a human rights barrister, practising from Ventnor. She is the acclaimed author of a number of previous books, 'The Thirty-Year Night', 'Re-Setting the World' and 'Olive Trees in Norway', as well as 'Feelan the Monster' for children.

She has three children and two grandchildren, and now lives on the Isle of Wight with her husband and their Old English Sheepdog, Basil.

Join the Bottomleys on their hilarious voyage to freedom of thought. The seas are rough with mischief, rife with mayhem, they meet rocks but free themselves back out onto the high seas. What they don't now is who is travelling with them, nor who is helping, who is hindering. A laugh a minute but flanked with questions we dare not ask.

But the answer lies here, hidden in humour.

LOKI'S GAME OF CARDS

by

TANYA WHITE

Chapter 1.

TO CALAMITY IN 40 MINUTES

The Bottomley family had just sat down for breakfast when a large man, giving his name as Loki, delivered a package containing two packs of cards, apparently from an anonymous sender. These preceded a catalogue of disaster, from the most innocent of beginnings.

"Rodney, can you collect Phoebe's eco nappies and change her, I have to leave early for the conference on Menopause in the Workplace."

"No, Geraldine, I can't."

"Why not, for heaven's sake?"

"Mum, you mustn't say that, it's offensive to religious people."

"Quiet, Jenny."

"Because I have to leave early too. I'm the only one there to man the office."

"Dad, you mustn't say 'man', it's 'person'"

"Shush."

"What about Carol, Trisha, Jeremy and Godfrey?"

"Carol is off on menopause leave. Trish is off on period leave. Jeremy is still on sick leave and won't be back until he's completed his transition to Jemima. And Godfrey is off having counselling, after he witnessed two dogs fighting causing him to suffer PTSD."

Their son Josh made the next smart suggestion. "Why don't you just wait for Nanny Bligh to arrive? She can change Phoebe."

"What?" Geraldine was hyperventilating. "You can't leave Phoebe in a dirty nappy!"

"Why not?"

Geraldine's anger management course hadn't worked. Josh received a large dose of abuse with his porridge.

"Don't talk to our son like that."

"Oh, actually…"

"Yes, Geraldine?"

"Just got a message from Nanny Bligh, hang on…"

Fortunately Geraldine's thoughts only manifested in her facial expression. Her words revealed the total opposite. "Nanny says she can't come, because when the tube train jerked a man held her back."

"Why?"

"To stop her falling, Rod."

"So what's the problem?"

"Nanny felt her personal space was invaded, and she's on her way to the police station to report him. She says he shouldn't have touched her."

"You mean he should have let her fall?" Josh smirked as he took up the baton, only for Jenny to rise to the bait.

"It's disgusting! No man should ever touch a woman without permission."

Josh would have been incensed but having been raised in a world of wokery he'd become sensitised. Anyway, calm logic seemed to be a better weapon. He continued.

"Ok, Jen. So, if a female is about to die, you can't resuscitate her? If she's about to fall and break a leg, you can't catch her? I know, we've had lessons in school – can't hold hands without permission, can't say this, can't say that – and you call us boys morons!"

Rodney got back on track. "Geraldine, you'd better phone your sister, Harriet, see if she can help out."

"Doubt it. She's incredibly busy in the Ministry of Re-writes. Do you realize how much skill is involved in re-writing the Oxford English Dictionary to ensure it doesn't have words which could be found offensive?"

Phoebe was in great discomfort, manifested by a continuous high-pitched scream. Resigned to being late, Geraldine went to get the eco nappies from the dryer. At least, she thought Rodders had the presence of mind to put them in to dry but... Phoebe's cries were hitting a crescendo when they were joined by Geraldine's vocals.

"You've bloody shrunk them! You put them on too high. What the f***!!"

Jenny piped up at the wrong moment. "Mummy, you mustn't say those words. Teacher says people who use that language can't express themselves properly."

Carrying a set of cloth nappies that wouldn't fit a Barbie doll, Geraldine slammed them down on the breakfast table. The momentum caused the spilling of the milk, orange juice and porridge, spreading into every hole and corner. The whole family needed a change of clothing. Rodney was despatched to purchase some (non-eco) throwaway nappies, though only after enduring a lecture from Jenny about how they were evil and destroying the planet.

Rodney got creative.

"What are you doing?"

"Mum, these cards have got 8 jokers."

"Don't interrupt, Jenny. Geraldine, it'll take me at least an hour through the traffic to get nappies, so I'm improvising something. There."

He took Phoebe, now hysterical, removed the overladen nappy, sodden and soiled, dropping it on the floor, and gently eased her into a pair of Jenny's pants, filled with kitchen roll encased in a large layer of Kleenex.

"Job done...rushing off now...Aaaagh!"

Rodney had just put his foot on the soiled nappy and slipped on the flagstone floor, knocking his head and cutting his hand on the broken crockery, bleeding into the nappy.

"Oh my God! Are you OK?"

"Mummy", Jenny now put a metaphorical foot in it "you mustn't say that, it's offensive to religious people."

Geraldine phoned 111. "Please hold, your call is important to us, someone will be with you shortly... you are currently number 2020 in the queue...did you know that you can find answers to most questions on our website..." then the background music cut in again.

Rodney stirred. "I'm all right, honestly, Josh, give me a hand."

Chapter 2.

THE OFFICE

Resigned to staying off work as a police administrator, Geraldine dispatched Jenny and Josh to school and settled down to clear up. Then the bell rang. She wondered whether she could pretend she was not in, but the window was open and Phoebe was crying, mirroring the chaos inside. Geraldine opened the door and stood, horror-struck. She tried to smile but it looked like an evil smirk. It was the Health Visitor on her routine visit.

"Hello Geraldine. You look...um...are you OK?"

"A bit hectic right now, Betsy. Would you mind coming back next week?"

"I can hear Phoebe. She does sound distressed."

Betsy was a well-built, determined middle-aged woman. She had seen it all, or so she thought. The cries and the smell rang alarm bells. She pushed past Geraldine into the kitchen-diner. Shocked and stunned she surveyed the blood and excrement intermingled with broken crockery and spilt food.

"Let me take Phoebe. Come on, my little one, why are you crying now?"

As she picked Phoebe up from the high chair it became clear that the makeshift nappy had not worked in any way, shape or form.

"Geraldine, what's going on here?"

"Well, Rodders shrunk the nappies. I was so cross with him!"

"But where's that blood come from?"

"It's Rodders'"

Betsy put 2 and 2 together and wondered if Geraldine had murdered him, looking at the carnage. She pondered her own safety, momentarily, mind. Her ample build compared to Geraldine's scrawny carcase was a comfort in that respect.

"Where is he now?"

"At work. I called 111 but didn't wait."

Betsy was starting a hot flush when she realized that the remaining contents of Phoebe's nappy had dispersed over her new M & S pinafore dress.

"I'm sorry, Geraldine, but I am concerned about Phoebe's welfare and I should like to see your husband."

Rodney had just arrived at the office when his secretary, Trudy, rushed over.

"Can I have a coffee, Trud?"

"We must speak first, it's urgent. Max Weybridge Bunter just came in. Yes, in person. He was furious, said our timber business was a shambles...he said he'd have no option but to cancel...6 months' wait and no deliveries...the fat pack houses should have been up by now."

"But Trud, the timber was despatched in part to Up Yours Delivery Services back in March. What happened?"

"I made enquiries. Apparently, all their drivers were off."

"Why?"

"One was on maternity leave, another on paternity leave, one had hurt herself moving the timber to the vehicle...well, she was that tiny one...another was on a training course, another at a disciplinary hearing..."

"All right, enough. I'll phone Bunty and eat humble pie."

"Not yet, Rodney. There's an urgent call from your wife."

Chapter 3

THE SCHOOL INSET DAY

"Josh, where is everyone?"

"I don't know, Jenny. Hang on, I think I can see a teacher...yes, let's go up there to the assembly room."

"Gosh, you're right, all the teachers and Headmaster Granger...all the teachers, no kids...must be an inset day and Mum forgot!"

Jenny thought for a moment.

"Don't fancy going back home to that mayhem, Josh."

"Why don't we listen in?"

"How?"

"Go in through Class B, down the stairs, through the corridor and below to the gym. It's just under the assembly room, the floorboards are not soundproof above."

Jenny and Josh expected a little mild entertainment. What they got was dynamite. Early on they recorded the gold dust on their phones, listening intently to the Headmaster speaking.

"We all just have to improvise. The Ministry of Education is still trying to revise the Bible. It's long and hard, but we cannot allow our pupils to read such violent stuff. It could cause them distress and anxiety. Trigger warnings are just not enough. For instance, what about Abraham being told by God to sacrifice his soon, so he ties him up, puts him on the altar, gets the knife. Or when Pharaoh won't let the children of Israel leave

Egypt, God sends 11 plagues and then sends an angel to kill every first-born child. Or Jephthah, sacrificing his daughter. Or Herod killing all the newborn babies. Yes, Mrs Melons, oh, sorry, Ms Melons...er...no...er...Melons?"

"How can you re-write the Bible?"

"Well, take Abraham's story. Perhaps he could be asked to stop his son's pocket money for a week, or send him to sit on the naughty step. Whatever, just lose the knife."

"Yes, Mr Granger...er...I mean, just Granger."

"Headmaster, as head of the biology department, I can say for all of us here that the new curriculum is just impossible."

"Why?"

"We are no longer permitted to use the notion of men and women, nor he and she. When depicting anatomy, God damn it, we refer to some 'in-between, neither male nor female' and we have to describe the reproductive organs of 'ze'. The kids are going to be totally confused. As for sex education, trying to teach that using unisex terminology is going to be impossible. Sorry, we just can't."

"There's no such word as 'can't'. We all have to find ways of stepping up into the new era of social responsibility. Yes, Faulkes, don't tell me, problems in history?"

"Wouldn't say problems, rather, catastrophe. We leave out references to slavery in case it upsets white people. We denigrate Churchill because he is now deemed racist. We exclude swathes of historical data because it could cause the kids distress. And half the history books are banned because they contain potentially offensive or racist terminology. So are we to represent a false view of history? The whole point of the subject is to learn the facts so that we can learn from old mistakes."

The English teacher, Mary Rowbotham, intervened.

"Hear hear. With literature most is trigger alarmed or banned. How do you read a poem and teach flow, creativity and metaphor with a trigger warning at the beginning of every sentence? Wasn't it Hitler who banned books?"

Granger understood the problems all too well. He was finding it hard to adapt and often committed social faux pas, but he had no choice but to lead the Lion School in accordance with educational protocol. Or did he have a choice? It was the physics master, Abdul Isaac Barnsley, who laid dynamite at everyone's feet.

Abdul's credentials were the personification of political correctness and a triumph for détente. Born to an English father and Jewish mother, with Muslim grandparents, he was married to a Scottish-born Ukrainian wife and had produced five very international offspring.

"Headmaster, enough. Look over there at the school's coat of arms and motto – 'Magna est Veritas et Praevalet', mighty is the truth and it prevails. We must take a stand for the sake of the children."

There was rapturous applause from the whole teaching staff. All eyes were on the Headmaster. The room filled with a powerful intensity. At last he spoke.

"I understand why we should take a stand. But how, and when? It's not feasible."

"Suppose" Abdul interjected "we begin by canvassing the parents. Sound them out. Then maybe a press release…meanwhile continuing the conventional curriculum."

"Ofsted will shut us down."

"They have to write a report first, Headmaster, and my brother is a top Government computer nerd."

"What's that got to do with anything?"

"Headmaster, not yet...'need-to-know' basis".

Chapter 4.

THE SCALPEL

Rodney had just finished reassuring the Health Visitor that Geraldine was not trying to murder him and that a child protection order was not needed, and having been offered a dustpan and brush she finally left. At that moment Rodney's brother, Felix, telephoned.

"Hi, just touching base, BBQ Saturday?"

"Please, not now, mayhem here."

"Anything I can do? I've got an op to do this afternoon but my evening, later, is free."

"An extra pair of hands and a listening ear would be great."

Feeling righteous and virtuous Felix proceeded the Ninja Hospital to perform a minor op, one that couldn't be easier. All scrubbed up, he entered the operating theatre and began.

"Scalpel."

Nurse Gloria did not pass a scalpel. He spoke louder.

"Scalpel."

Still nothing.

"For fuck's sake..."

"Felix, you must say 'Please may I have the scalpel?' Politeness costs nothing."

The second theatre nurse piped up.

"She's quite right. You can't speak to staff like that. We'll report you for sex discrimination."

"The bloody anaesthetic will wear off at this rate. Please give me the fucking scalpel!"

"That's it." Gloria downed tools, at least she would have done if she'd picked them up in the first place, and was promptly copied by the second nurse.

"We are going to Human Resources to lodge a complaint."

"What about the bloody patient?"

Felix operated alone, without assistance. Fuming, he called porter Johnson to remove the patient to the ward. At least, he thought, he'd see his brother shortly.

"Felix, you're wanted in Operating Theatre 5."

"What? I can't, Sister, I was only scheduled for this one."

"It's urgent."

"But Mohammed is on Ops 5."

"He can't, and you're needed now."

Scrubbing up and assembling the team Felix spat out "Why is Mohammed not doing it?"

"He has to go to the mosque for special prayers."

"Well, what about Jocelyn? She hasn't done any ops today."

"She's at ante-natal classes."

"Philip? He's done nothing all week."

"He's with his wife at her ante-natal classes."

Felix resigned himself and got stuck in with his patient (quite literally).

"Please may I have the scalpel, Marian?"

"Oh Felix, you don't have to stand on the politically correct politeness platform with me! I drank you under the table last month, remember?"

Felix remembered all right...he'd had the hots for Marian since last year's Christmas party...oh, those stockings...the beat on the heart monitor brought him back quickly.

"This one's doing well, Marian, nearly done...there. James, close up for me. Juia's taking over your slot now Marian, let's go and clean up."

"I say, Felix, do you want to get even...on the drinks front?"

"Give me a moment."

Felix phoned his brother, knew he'd understand, they were both very close.

"No problem, Felix, we'll meet up tomorrow. Lucky sod, saw her at your last barbecue...bloody stunning mate...although Geraldine reckoned there was something wrong with her. Too muscular, she said. Still, I reckon it was a touch of the old green eye. You get lucky mate, have some fun for me."

Marian and Felix were ad idem on politics, love, life the world. They were a bit old for clubbing but hey...

"Darling, let's go back to mine for a chaser, this is just too noisy."

"Ok Felix, but you'll have to take the couch."

His face dropped.

"Just give me time, darling. Come on, quick, there's a cab."

Two chasers later…"Felix, I do love you, but we need to talk."

"Marian, we've talked all night."

"But Felix…"

He pulled her tightly into his arms in a warm passionate embrace. He was ecstatic…until he felt something stirring in her groin as well as his.

"What the fuck?" He pushed her away.

"I'm the same person, Felix, the mind you love. In another year my transition will be complete."

"You must be kidding if you think…"

"Felix, are you going to start being discriminatory and transphobic? If you are, I'm having you at the Tribunal. I get where Gloria is coming from. You're a bigot, a bastard!"

Chapter 5.

SECRETS AND LIES

"Josh, we mustn't tell anyone about this, we'll be in trouble for eavesdropping."

"Of course, Jenny. And, hey, it sounds like something big is going to happen, we don't want to scupper it. By the way, Jenny, you know how we can find those banned books they were on about? If Mum and Dad read them at our age, why can't we?"

"Yes, but we need money. They've got them in that old book store in Bridge Street, loads of them, Nietzsche, Kipling...anyway, let's get back. We'll say we've been to Nan's"

Rodney's worst fears had come to fruition. His accountant had read the last rites. Tomorrow would be the meeting at Bolder's Bank. The carpet was likely to be pulled. Until then, he was not going to worry Geraldine, who'd just made a wonderful family meal.

"So then, Jenny, Josh, have a good time at Nan's?"

"Yeah" in unison.

They started to tuck into the Tofu Suprème, when the phone rang.

"Hello, is that Mrs Bottomley?"

"Yes."

"Please don't be alarmed, I'm Nurse Bembridge from the Allbright Hospital. Your mother will be fine, but she is going to need some help."

"What? She can't be ill. She runs an organic smallholding with my father. No chemicals, everything is natural and eco-friendly. They're as fit as fiddles. Anyway, my kids have just been there."

"Oh no! Please bring the children to hospital straight away...no...I'll arrange an ambulance. They'll need a stomach pump. There was botulinus in the blueberries. Your father only had a few, he's okay, but your mother had a bowlful. Did the children eat any?"

As the ambulance drew up Jenny and Josh's protestations were ignored. Only when Dr Bee Gee examined them were they pardoned.

Nanny Twitster was lying in Ward 3 on a saline drip, having imbibed, courtesy of the hospital, a number of unnatural substances, when Geraldine arrived.

"Don't worry. Rodders will arrange for some help for you and Dad on the farm, meanwhile you can stay with us. I absolutely insist."

Nanny Twitster's heart monitor beeped.

Rodney wasn't sure he could afford next month's food bill, never mind paying for a farm hand. Geraldine would have to be told.

Geraldine grabbed a sneaky gin and tonic, feeling overwhelmed. Then the mobile rang.

"Hello Geraldine, it's Bonnie from HR. I notice you have been off work without proper approval. Just touching base. Is everything okay?"

"Just a few domestic issues, I shall need a little more time."

"I'm so sorry, Geraldine, but there's no-one to deputise for you. Sarah is on disciplinary leave."

"Why, Bonnie? Sarah is a stickler for all rules and regulations, her nickname is Goody Two-shoes."

"Well I suppose I can tell you, it's not breaching data protection, the court case is in the public domain now."

"What?"

"She's being prosecuted by the RSPCA for cruelty to an animal. Her dachshund, actually."

"But Bonny, that's ridiculous. She has no family, that dog is her soulmate. She dotes on it. It's pampered, groomed, loved and adored. She even cooks it special, homemade vegan meals."

"Er, that's the problem Gerry. The vegan diet caused the dog cramps, exhaustion and malnutrition. When she took it to the vet he reported her. The prosecution are saying she must have known what she was doing."

"But she's vegan. She hates the idea of meat eating. Anway, Maureen can manage, surely?"

"No, she's on sick leave, suffering from mental stress after witnessing a traumatic event."

"What event?"

"She was walking down Rosebud Avenue when she witnessed a car running over a pigeon. The image haunted her waking hours and dreams, the blood and the carcase on the road, the extinction of life, it was all too much."

Geraldine bit her tongue, kept her thoughts totally private. Fuming, she relented. Bonnie had her way.

Rodney was late for his meeting with Lee Myers at Bolder's (Caring for You) People's Bank.

"So sorry I'm late, lots of work at the office."

Lee Myers had just returned from his customer care course, equipped with a broad smile and a firm handshake. He began.

"Here at the Caring Bank we take a holistic view. It's not about money, it's about people's lives. We aim to help our customers through thick and thin. Hard times come and go. We stand together, all of us, a smorgasbord of genders, nationalities, religions, all together, our strength s born from our strong sense of compassion and care."

"That's very reassuring Mr Myers. I'm afraid I come today in hard times and will need a £50,000 facility to tide the business over in anticipation of our next contract."

"I don't see any details of a future contract from the paperwork, Mr Bottomley, and before the meeting I phoned your major buyer to confirm the trading only to be told he'd taken his business elsewhere."

"Yes, you see we had a staff hiatus at the time, but that's now resolved. I am confident of arranging new contracts shortly."

"Unfortunately, Mr Bottomley, there is a dividing line between a holistic approach bathed in compassion and negligent use of the bank's money. It is one thing to help a struggling business when a brighter future is commercially viable but another thing altogether to throw money at a haemorrhaging enterprise. To do so would simply be enabling the misfortune to continue, to eke out the pain. That would be quite improper."

"Hello, Nanny Bligh? It's Geraldine here."

"Hi, how are you?"

"Not too good. I really need you over here tomorrow early. I have to get back to work."

"Oh, I'm so sorry, but didn't you get the letter from my counsellor?"

"What, the one that said you are still suffering from stress due to the train incident?"

"Yes, that's it. Brigitte, my counsellor, feels that I need more meditation time. I need to reflect, to understand. I was so upset when the police refused to investigate. I have an ongoing complaint with the police department. I need closure before I am able to concentrate on work."

"Now look here, Bligh, should the man have let you fall and break your neck? For god's sake pull yourself together and stop wallowing. If you're not back here first thing you're sacked!"

"Right, that's it, Geraldine. After all I've done for you. You can expect my solicitors to be in touch with a claim for unfair dismissal, with aggravated damages. You've made my stress and anxiety far worse now."

"You stupid cow, you've done nothing for me except sponge...days off for bad period days...off for stubbing your big toe...won't do any washing or cleaning up because 'I'm a Nanny, not a cleaner'. Expect me to get all the food and toys ready for you. All you do is sit here or go out to coffee shops. What baby sitting you do is sub-standard, all done when you're on bloody Twitter. So sod off."

Geraldine felt on reflection that her £10,000 private anger management course had been a total rip-off.

Chapter 6.

SOBRIETY

Rodney was in the Frolics Arms with Felix. After 4 pints and 4 chasers apiece, the stiff upper lips began sagging.

"Look, Rodders, you must have a bit of equity in that house of yours by now."

"Nope...remortgaged and into negative equity now."

Silence.

"Okay, this is what I can do. I've no family, been on high pay for years, yes, I'm suspended without pay at the moment but there's a lot of padding in various financial baskets. As for the London penthouse, well, I'm tired of all that life now, Rodders...wine, women (and some in-betweens) constant noise and bustle, even the electric Porsche is soulless, drives like a geriatric on wheels. I just have my gorgeous nephew and nieces thanks to you and Geraldine. No, my mind's made up. No time like the present so come on, bank details Rodders, now."

"Can't do that bro, where would you live? What happens if you can't get re-employed? Discrimination cases going pear-shaped means the scrapheap...it's not happening."

"Come on Rods, we've been close since childhood. It's not about you alone, it's my nieces and nephew I'll be damned if they end up without a decent roof over their heads. And what about my visits? I love playing with them...part of the family and all that. Truth is, I'm lonely. I can't deal with love in a politically correct climate...keep getting it wrong, and some! Remember Jasmine?"

"Yeah, I thought that one was serious."

"It ended on a moonlit walk. Starry skies, warm summer night, pulled her close, passionate kiss. That was it. She told me I should have asked her permission first before kissing her. So I kissed her again, I thought she was joking. That's how I ended up in A & E with a broken wrist...a black belt judo instructor, our Jasmine. Bloody attacked me, left me on the promenade and buggered off. Hell, if it wasn't two decent passers-by, a couple of teenagers, would you believe, it could have been worse. Goddammit, Marina left me because I formally asked for permission to hold her, she told me I was totally unromantic, lacked impulse and spontaneity and resembled a boring old fart. So please, Rodders, let me help."

"Bro, there is one basis on which I would consider accepting. We have 2 spare rooms, 3 if we use the study, which is no longer need now the caring bank has pulled the plug. Why not really be part of the family? Stay with us. Geraldine and the kids adore you, you know that."

Geraldine had put the kids to bed and settled down to a few snifters when the bloody mobile rang again.

51

"Hi, it's Harriet, I don't know who to turn to, I've been sacked!"

"Why?"

"The Ministry of Rewrites said I was being totally insubordinate because I refused to ban a whole list of books, from Black Beauty (triggering name) and The Hound of the Baskervilles (too scary, and anti-dog) to The Origin of Species (no awareness of transgender issues) and virtually everything on science or history written by dead white men (don't ask!) Then I wouldn't delete masses of the Oxford English Dictionary as triggering (slavery) or racist (denigration) or offensive (male and female). It means I can't pay my rent Geraldine. Can you put me up until I can find my feet?"

"Actually, Harriet, that would work brilliantly. We've just lost Nanny Bligh. You could sort the kids. I know you're crazy over Phoebe. Or, um, would it cramp your love life?"

"No, darling, I'm fed up with men. They behave like women these days, 'please may I hold your hand', they don't stand up or give up a seat, don't care who enters the room first, no opening car doors, and as for sex...well, it's so sanitized and formal, permission confirmed first, in writing – they're worried they might read the wrong vibes – no first move. Frankly, Gerry, I'd rather have a pot of Haagen Daas in front of an old film...think Marlon Brando, Richard Burton, Sean Connery...God, remember darling, real men! Do you know, they shave their chests now...and more...might as well have a woman."

Geraldine hadn't laughed so much in months. Tears of laughter were streaming down her face when Rodney returned. More alcohol was imbibed, and truths were revealed, followed by more laughter, together this time, as they both snatched at the same thought – Felix and Harriet, the perfect couple.

With 3 adults to one baby and 2 teenagers, Geraldine went to work with a spring in her step.

Chapter 7.

RODNEY'S NEW ROLE

Rodney was relishing his role as house husband. He particularly enjoyed playdates at young mummies' houses. He was plied with coffee and nibbles and dispensed wise counsel to all the mothers' private love issues, but more, he loved talking about fashion.

"I think it's wonderful that women should wear clothes which reveal their true personality" he said, to rapturous applause, but thought privately that it was wonderful that boob tubes and minis were so 'now'. He was like a child in a sweet shop.

"Thank you, Rodders, so much." Julia was head of the 'women's right to flaunt what you like' group. "I was so cross with that awful headmaster from Frumpbridge School who said that mums should set an example to their girls by dressing in a lady-like fashion. How dare he."

"Absolutely, Julia. I thought that silk jimmy set you wore the other day was absolutely divine, so artistic." (Rodders receiving more praise...Rodders thinking 'no underwear underneath...rapture'.)

"Well, I don't want to be a bore."

"Yes, Grace?"

"My eldest son, Brian, he says he can't focus on his work when he sits next to your Lily, Julia. He says her red bra shows through the white blouse and he can see everything when she climbs the school stairs!"

Oh dear, cat fight ensued. Rodney knew Josh had problems focussing for similar reasons, and no way would he let Jenny attend school in anything other than formal attire. He was wrestling with his conscience when suddenly he realised all their eyes were on him, demanding a man's view. He was on the spot now.

"From a biological and scientific view, a teenage boy is like a car with an accelerator and no brakes. His brain is firing impulses which he curbs with great hardship. Similarly, a teenage girl often feels ostracized if she does not follow peer pressures. She may want to dress conservatively but feel unable so to do, which is as bad as being prevented from dressing as one pleases. As an adult, with a fully developed brain, no raging hormones, no allegiance to peer pressures and so forth, the choice is free. For teenagers it is not. The reasoning behind school uniform is fundamentally to ensure that everyone will fit in, in terms of money, social status, style and so forth, so our young fireballs can be steadied along to focus on their education. Put this another way, ladies. How would you feel if you were working in a small room on a serious presentation you had only 2 hours to complete, bear with me, it requires all your attention, all your focus, but sitting opposite you is Brad Pitt wearing only a pair of silk boxers. Would your focus be impaired?"

There was a long silence, then muttering which Rodney couldn't make out. Then Julia stood up.

"I propose we make Rodney chairperson of our women's group, with immediate effect." There was rapturous applause.

Rodney's utter delight was totally quashed the next time he met the young mummies. The decadent dress style had morphed into utter frump, with flared jeans, wide jackets, trainers and sweatshirts.

The headmaster at Frumpbridge School was delighted.

Chapter 8.

OFSTED AND THE LION

"Gerry, have you seen this letter from Godfrey Granger?"

Rodney re-read it with Geraldine:

Dear Parents,

In the interests of our pupils, we have decided to take a stand on what can only be described as an Orwellian culture, dictated to us by the Ministry of Abridged Education. Each Department Head has voiced his or her concerns, and I have set out some of those concerns below:

1. Religious Education.

The Bible has been so distorted, with deletions, changes, trigger warnings and such like that it has metamorphosised into something entirely different. We cannot teach core stories in case they offend, or show violence, or other undesirable aspects. For example, the creation story offends by displaying male superiority over women, and human superiority over animals, while the Christmas story involves inter-species sex, child-birth in wholly insanitary conditions and the arrival of strange men with gifts, all utterly undesirable. If even these have to be censored you can imagine what happens to the fall of Jericho, or David and Goliath, or other more violent passages. We mention this first because so many of you will be more familiar with it, but the same is true for the Torah, the Koran, the Book of Mormon and Buddhist and Hindu texts. We cannot therefore teach our pupils what these really say.

2. Literature.

A long list of books has been banned, as showing too much violence, discrimination, offensive attitudes and so on. These include Oliver Twist (for anti-semitism), War and Peace (far too violent), 20 Years a Slave (because it might trigger discomfort in white pupils) Robinson Crusoe (for racism), Gulliver's Travels (hostility to differently-sized people) and the War poets, who are far too upsetting. The only Shakespeare we may teach is As You Like It (without the wrestling match) – even A Midsummer Night's

Dream offends with the Mechanicals as class stereotypes. 1984 is also banned, presumably because it's too revealing. The full list is enormous, and the children are being cut off from what should be their cultural heritage.

3. History.

History is the study of what happened in the past and why, and inevitably a great deal of it is about the use of force by individuals, groups and nations to gain power. Once we are not allowed to teach the children about bad things that happened in the past, because they may upset or offend, what we can teach ceases to be the truth. That almost every history book written before the last 10 years or so is banned is merely an aspect of the problem, that if we can't teach the facts, we are not teaching history.

4. Biology.

"Male" and "Female" terminology is now banned, as exclusivist, transphobic and offensive. An inevitable consequence is that the accurate teaching of anatomy, sexual reproduction, and indeed most of biology, becomes impossible. And for the great majority of the pupils, who are perfectly and comfortably aware that they themselves are, as the case may be, male or female, the lessons become both confusing and absurd.

These are, as noted above, just some examples. The reality is that we are being forced to lie to our pupils, by omission and sometimes directly, in what we teach them.

Nor is that the only problem. We are also forced to mollycoddle them, shielding them from anything which others think might cause them any level of upset, that they are likely to grow up quite unable to recognize real dangers, or to stand up for themselves against any hostile behaviour. We can, for instance, no longer take them on camping holidays because of the envisaged 'dangers'. I enclose a copy of the current Ministry of Abridged Education Guidelines, which you will see include:

1. Risk of rain, leading the children to get wet, with the possibility of pneumonia;

2. Risk of snake or insect bites, causing itching, followed by scratching, resulting in sepsis;

3. Risk of poorly-cooked food causing stomach aches, leading to gastroenteritis;

4. Risk from campfires, causing burns and/or encouraging children to become arsonists;

5. Sleeping in tents on the ground, with risk of back-ache and long-term lumbar problems;

6. Being out in the wilds at night, causing children to be fearful.

Most of our canteen staff have resigned, as you know, and children now have to bring in their own food for lunch. This was because the staff were unable, on the small budget available, to offer in suitable quantities the menus demanded, which were vegan 10%, vegetarian 15%, kosher 7.5%, halal 7.5%, none of the foregoing 60%, but within that last category a suitable proportion had to be organic, or dairy free, or grain-free or nut-free or egg-free or free of all these.

As you are also aware, discipline has been an issue. We do not and will never endorse corporal punishment. We do, however, feel like toothless dogs when we are not even allowed (by the Ministry of Abridged Education, not by you parents) to require a pupil to stay behind for 20 minutes after-school detention, under the supervision of a teacher, where apologies and such like can be written. Instead, we have to follow prescriptions which I would describe as psychobabble and which I strongly believe are in fact psychologically harmful. We believe in "You have misbehaved and you now have detention", after which the matter is closed, rather than "Tell me why you did that. It was so wrong. You must think about it, ruminate on it, and we shall speak again tomorrow", when the matter is not closed, and the pupil probably thinks we are idiots.

We ask you for your vote of confidence, to stand with the school, uphold its motto, and allow our children the freedom to explore, the freedom to be children, the freedom to learn and the freedom to make mistakes, and not to be constantly watched, analysed, confused and imprisoned in a mental and physical bubble of untruths.

RSVP.

Godfrey Granger found the full backing from the parents the catalyst he needed to face the Ofsted invasion. They came, they rampaged through every cabinet, class, hall and cupboard. As they marched out from the Lion School Abdul made his move.

"Excuse me, Mr Abdul Isaac Barnsley, how do you do?" He held out his hand. "I have to ask you to sign the visitors' book here; a formality, but nevertheless…"

"Sorry, we are in a rush."

"How rude. You refuse to shake my hand and do us the courtesy of a visitor's signature. Is this because of my name…or the colour of my skin?"

The Ofsted inspectors were alert to the repercussions of any allegation, even if baseless, of racial discrimination. So Mr Peasbody and Mrs Bollockson decided that back-saving was the better part of valour. Abdul's hand was firmly shaken, and his visitors' book signed.

"Olav, it's Abdul, need an urgent meet bro, you owe me one, remember? I'll come up your way, meet you at the Dodger's Inn at 1 pm."

Two swift halves later, Olav had his remit from Abdul. Holding the fake report, endorsed with forged signatures, he reluctantly agreed to prostitute his genius-level computer skills in the interests of the greater good, and because he owed Abdul big-time – think card counting!

By the next morning the press was buzzing, and the Ministry of Abridged Education was erupting. The Bottomleys, like the rest of the country, couldn't believe the headlines in the papers.

'An anonymous source has leaked the main tenets of the Ofsted report into the Lion School, notorious for its steadfast defiance of what it has called the defiling of literature, religion and science. We set out the main part of the report:

This report has been compiled with the full consent and cooperation of the Lion School.

1. Its academic success is outstanding.

2. The pupils are happy, well-grounded and fit.

3. Sports are encouraged. We note that the games staff do not limit artificially the scope for physical excellence for fear of the odd bruise or sprain.

4. The children are mentally and physically enriched by regular camping excursions, where they learn invaluable life skills, including building camps, making fires, and foraging, and enjoy outdoor pursuits and singsongs round the campfire.

5. By being allowed in age-appropriate classes to devour the unabridged jewels of great literature their creative skills have grown and flourished, far exceeding their counterparts in other schools who have been served with a diet abridged and damped-down prose and verse.

6. Their understanding of religion is superior to those who have had to learn with half the texts redacted out.

7. They respect their teachers and relate well within peer groups. Discipline is rarely a problem. They are not afraid to misbehave and do not fear detention, but they respect the boundaries for the most part.

8. The teachers show compassion and understanding when teaching delicate subjects involving, for instance, history of wars or inter-

racial violence and the like. The emphasis is to learn from the mistakes of mankind so that they will not be repeated, rather than redacting them out and letting them happen again.

9.   This is all done in an age-appropriate manner.

Signed   Mrs Bollockson

Mr Peasbody

Mrs Bollockson was unavailable for comment, having had some sort of breakdown and been sectioned under the Mental Health Act 1983. Mr Peasbody was also unavailable for comment, having imbibed so much whisky that he had to be rushed to A & E to have his stomach pumped.

A tsunami of parents from schools everywhere was on the rampage, demanding that their children have the same benefits as the pupils at the Lion School, leading to an emergency meeting of the Headteachers' union. They too were in complete agreement, armed with universal support. There was no stopping them now. The Chair rose to give a closing call to arms.

"Fellow Heads, we must fight together.

We will fight in the classrooms, we will fight in the gyms, we will fight in the hallways and in the chapels. We will fight on the games pitches. We will never surrender!"

His Churchillian rhetoric met with rapturous applause.

Chapter 9.

THE POLICE FEDERATION

With so much excitement, Geraldine was almost relieved to be sitting at her desk at work. Josh and Jenny were like dynamite, Felix and Harriet were like teenage lovebirds, Rodders had been dancing to Abba while doing the housework and playing supernanny in his pink apron, and Nana Twitster was too much on form.

"Good morning Gerry. I want you to be in charge of the new police initiative. They have been trained and are ready to roll but you have to oversee the correct numbers."

Geraldine nodded. She wasn't up to speed, had no idea what he was talking about, but she winged it.

"You understand the reasoning, don't you? I know it's hard to stomach, flies in the face of civil liberties and all that, but what else can we do, lest we be accused of tyrannical racism? I think Professor Knowland's guidance says it all. Obviously, official secrets and all that, if this got out we'd all be given a rocket up our arses and sent to Mars!"

Not having a clue what he was on about, she played along.

"Oh yes, of course, Superintendent. I fully appreciate the full issue and overriding policy. The data analysis speaks volumes."

"I'll leave it in your more than capable hands then. Oh yes, everyone's back now so delegate freely. Cheerio."

Quickly she logged on and found the Police Incentive Remit and Guidelines.

'Data shows an overrepresentation of arrests of non-white persons, for some time. This has caused widespread criticism that the force is inherently racist. This criticism is widely reported across parties and among the general population. Possible disorder, rioting and even anarchy is forecast if this concern is not addressed. We have therefore approved the introduction of positive discrimination to rebalance the figures, as a crude overview only. Please appreciate that there are numerous complex nuances of a social, economic and psychological nature, which are detailed I Appendix 4(f). In practice, if an officer arrests someone from a minority ethnic background a corresponding arrest of a white person must also be made, irrespective of the existence of any reasonable grounds so to do. This must be like for like. If the minority ethnic person is old the white person must also be old, and similarly for other ages or particular characteristics. These arrests will be closely monitored.'

Geraldine almost choked on her coffee. This was utterly absurd. She stood up and marched to the Superintendent's door. Then she stopped and bowed her head in shame. She remembered that she was the only breadwinner right now in the whole family. Felix had injected a large amount of cash, but they were getting through it faster than she would like. She would have to swallow everything she stood for, rights, liberty, freedoms, safety, and that thought choked her mentally.

Meanwhile, Millie (Nana Twitster) decided to take the train up to the Smoke with her dear old friend Sarah Bond. They felt they deserved a little foraging in Fortnums. They would start with lunch, then a little cheeky shopping. They couldn't really afford it, certainly shouldn't, but...

DS Perkins and PC Dribble had just successfully arrested the two Bond Street Mafia Grans, notorious for forgery and blackmail – at the minor end of such crimes perhaps, but worth arresting. They had just logged in the two women, Ola Oluwusola and Stella Abegona, at the station, when the Superintendent came out and demanded that they go straight back and find two counterparts, of white origin, in keeping with the new guidelines.

"Bloody ridiculous, Dribble. In the old days we'd get a pat on the back and bought a round, now it's go out and arrest an innocent to balance the books!"

"Too right. I didn't join the force for this lark, mate. Look, I have an idea. We can't disobey – mortgages to pay, kids to feed – we can't leak it to the press, that's even worse, but we could..."

"Spit it out, Dribble, I'm all ears."

"Suppose we obey to the letter. I mean, arrest obvious innocents for totally spurious reasons, cause a rumpus like, a bit like those school masters."

"I'm getting your drift, Dribble. Yes, I'm game. Let's start with Fortnums restaurant, it's on our patch, right?"

Nana Twitster and Sarah were engrossed in chatter, enjoying their cappuccino and chocolate fudge dessert when Sarah looked up.

"Millie, those policemen are looking at us."

Sarah put her hand in her pocket. At that point DS Perkins and PC Dribble came over.

"We are arresting both of you for attempted breach of the peace. I must caution you..."

"How?" said Millie and Sarah in unison.

"We saw you (this was addressed to Sarah) putting your right hand in your pocket. I must caution you..."

At this point DS Perkins was drowned out by riotous laughter all round the restaurant. The waiter arrived with the bill. PC Dribble whispered something about expenses and reclaiming, and next thing, they paid the bill. DS Perkins then said to them both "I'm afraid you have to come with us to the police station", and finally got to complete the formal caution, "You do not have to say anything, but if you fail to mention when questioned something on which you later rely in court it may harm your defence."

PC Dribble added apologetically "We will drive you, please come."

A number of people in the restaurant protested. An older gentleman by the name of Frode Forseti, his jacket adorned with medals, stood up, chivalry personified.

"How dare you? My wife is telephoning our son right now, he is a criminal KC. The police force should prepare to empty its pockets on a large compensation claim. The further you go with this, the larger the claim. Think about it."

Millie and Sarah thought too. Sarah couldn't resist.

"Are you saying that if they make us go to the station we claim more, and if they put us in a cell, even more?"

"Absolutely."

Millie and Sarah felt they could use a few bob, both having millionaire's tastes and a fish and chip income.

Millie whispered to the old gentleman, who then asked PC Dribble "To which station are you taking them?"

"Kensington."

His wife called out "Leif, that's our son ladies, he'll be down at the station with you in a couple of hours. Meanwhile, I'll tip off the press."

Millie and Sarah were treated like royalty in the cells, special orders delivered from Fortnums, it was far easier than their old boarding school. Rusty as their maths was, the damages for wrongful arrest and false imprisonment were mounting by the minute, and then there was the chance of offers of money for exclusives...

Word spread fast, finally reaching Geraldine. That was too much. Her mother had been good to her and had struggled to make sure she had the best. No, she was done with wrestling with her conscience. She phoned Reuters, and it wasn't just a leak, it was a flood.

The press had the proverbial field day:

Daily Mail – 'Police crackdown on innocent white grannies';

The Times – 'Police Federation policy to arrest palpably innocent white people, from children to grandparents, to hide internal racism';

The Financial Times – 'Police forces face bankruptcy over wrongful arrest compensation claims';

The Guardian – 'The intentional arrest of innocent people to camouflage police racism drives a horse and cart through the rule of law';

The Independent – 'Exclusive – the story of the suffering of two poor, innocent lady pensioners and the stress, strain, indignity, humiliation, fear, even terror inflicted on these two elderly pillars of the community by their public and wrongful arrest and subsequent incarceration. This is the shocking story of Sarah and Millie, and it happened in the United Kingdom in the 21st century.'

Millie and Sarah couldn't believe how easy it was to make £500,000.

Chapter 10.

FALSE PERCEPTIONS

Rodney was on form. He'd just collected Jenny and Josh from school, stopping at the park with Phoebe en route, his thoughts filled with new Delia Smith recipes.

Harriet and Felix were just finishing coffee when Felix noticed a couple of letters lying on the mantelpiece. Rodney had put them there that morning. He could tell from the envelopes what they were. Harriet knew the background.

"Please read them. I can't bear to."

"OK, here goes. This one's from the Employment Tribunal, that's Marian's sex discrimination claim. 'Conclusion. The Tribunal has concluded that it cannot be unlawful sex discrimination if a person intending to have consensual sex with a person of specific gender and sexual orientation declines to proceed on discovering that the other party is not in fact of that gender and orientation. There would be no consent. In any event, it would mean that a person would be guilty of discrimination if they refused to have sex with another person who had misrepresented to the first person what gender and/or sexual orientation the second person actually was. The claim is dismissed. Further, the Tribunal is taking the rare decision to make a costs order in favour of the respondent, and invites further written submissions on the appropriate amount.' And the second one is from the Internal Disciplinary Enquiry – that's Gloria's claim. 'The Panel are unanimous in finding that the Respondent, Felix Bottomley, did not discriminate as alleged or at all. Not saying 'please' and being brusque is impolite but we are not here to adjudicate on manners. We note that the Respondent's manner, as complained about, does not change whether he is addressing men, women or persons of some other gender, or persons of minority or majority ethnicity. We therefore rule that the Respondent be reinstated forthwith. We further advise that he seeks to adopt a more courteous manner in future.'"

"Harriet, I love you, this is wonderful."

"Come on Felix, got to celebrate...race you to your bedroom for a game of strip chess. You grab a couple of glasses, I've got a couple of bottles of champagne. They're all out."

Rodney was pleased to see that Phoebe hadn't woken when he removed her, still in the car seat and left her, still sleeping, in the lounge for a short spell while he got the house in order. He put on Geraldine's pink apron and muff cleaning gloves.

"Come on guys. Josh, you're on bathrooms, here's the spray. Jenny, floors."

"Come on Dad, I've got homework."

"So has Jenny. The sooner you start the sooner you'll finish."

"Dad, the phone's ringing. It's Mum's number flagged up."

"Pop it on speaker, Josh, my hands are full of flour and butter."

"Please leave a message after the tone…Rodders, I'm going to get the sack. I might even be prosecuted for breach of the Official Secrets Act and sent to jail. I'm okay, tell you all about it later. I might be early, I'm on my way back, but stopping off with Babs at the Old Oak so I might be a bit rat-arsed."

Rodney quickly the turned the phone message off with a buttery hand, while the kids looked anxious.

"Mum's joke, guys. She often uses it as an excuse to meet Babs."

Rodney was nervous. He burnt the pie and spilt the egg white. Phoebe woke, and was just reaching a crescendo when the doorbell rang.

"I'll get it," said Josh.

"Hello young man. Why are you wearing rubber gloves?"

"I've been made to clean the toilets."

"And I have to scrub the floors."

Betsy, the Health Visitor, had just popped round to close the file on the Bottomleys, having been long overdue. However...

"What's that screaming? I smell burning. Where's your Mum?"

"She's going to prison, but right now she's getting rat-arsed in the pub, isn't she Josh?"

Betsy felt palpitations and anxiety symptoms. She was trying slow breathing when Rodney appeared in a pink apron and pink muff gloves, with his face splattered with butter and flour. Then she heard primeval screaming from upstairs.

"What's going on?"

Betsy's mothering spirit rose up. She would protect the children. What first? She followed the shrieks, maybe a child was up there.

In their haste Felix and Harriet hadn't locked the bedroom door. Flinging it wide open, Betsy was horrified. Two grown people, totally naked, jumping up and down and with chess pieces coming out of...never mind, she closed the door quickly and ran to Phoebe.

"There, there. So bad to let little ones sleep in car seats. Now, Josh, Jenny, why aren't you doing your homework?"

"Dad makes us do chores."

"Slavery!", Betsy roared at Rodney.

At this point there was a commotion at the front door. In came Geraldine and Babs, very much under the influence and it was still only the afternoon. They sat down and both passed out, drunk. Felix had come downstairs, asking "Where's my scalpel?"

"Sorry mate" said Rodney "I borrowed it for the Delia chicken recipe."

"But I'm going back to work, I want the scalpel, where is it?"

Betsy only heard the word "scalpel".

Felix took one look at Geraldine and Babs and promptly turned them both to the recovery position. Then he called an ambulance. "They'll need stomach pumping", he smirked. Betsy thought the smirk positively evil.

"Sarah?"

"Yes, Millie?"

"Are you coming? I told you, I know our Gerry is in a financial mess. She thinks I don't know. I'm going to give her the good news that I'll help her out."

They proceeded to the Bottomleys. They were two minor celebrities now, between their triumphant release and their subsequent forays to Harvey Nicks. They were now fashion icons for the over-60s. They were followed by an entourage of reporters and fashion editors. They arrived at the same time as the ambulance, only to find themselves embroiled in another scoop. Betsy, overcome with fear, had grabbed the children and was at the open front door waving a bread knife at Felix and Rodney.

"You're all disgusting, depraved. I'm taking the children to a place of safety."

"No, we're not going. Give me Phoebe."

"Come on Josh, Jenny, you said you were slaves!"

"We said no such thing, Betsy...Phoebe's screaming."

The police arrived on cue. Betsy was sectioned under the Mental Health Act.

Chapter 11.

CALM BEFORE THE STORM

Jenny and Josh retired early, they felt they'd had more than enough adventures and the play station beckoned. Phoebe had settled nicely after a good feed. Geraldine, Rodney, Felix and Harriet were enjoying a Thai curry, courtesy of Rodney's new culinary skills. Harriet was the first to break the ice.

"I am so sorry guys, Felix and I were totally out of order, weren't we Felix?"

"Yes, too true. Look, I'm earning again now, I can rent somewhere with Harriet if you feel…"

"Absolutely not. You've been so kind and generous and the kids adore you both. We want you both to stay, don't we Rodders?"

"Too right. In fact, we were wondering if you wouldn't mind both babysitting tomorrow night so Gerry and I can have a break. It's all been a bit of a nightmare."

"Our pleasure" said Feix and Harriet together.

The next day Geraldine had finally finished her make-up and they were about to leave when there was a knock at the door.

"Good evening. I am DCI Brainstorm and this is DC Pennington. Here are our warrant cards. We are here to speak to Mrs Bottomley, may I ask if that is you?"

"Yes, Chief Inspector, what is it?"

"We have reason to believe, following an investigation, that you have purposely provided information in breach of the Official Secrets Act. I must ask you to accompany us to the police station for an interview" and he formally cautioned her.

It was past midnight when Geraldine was finally released on conditional bail.

"You really don't look well, Gerry."

"I know, Felix, I feel like shit."

He checked her vitals and wasn't happy with the results. He booked her in for a private consultation with Dr Toogood the following morning. Harriet phoned Nana Twitster for good measure.

Just when Geraldine was feeling lower than low, Nana Twitster appeared, with Leif Forseti, KC, MBE.

"Hello darling, meet Leif. I met his Dad in Fortnums, he's the one who came to the police station to help me out. Now this lovely gentleman is here to help you."

"Thank you, Leif, but it's hopeless. I did breach the Act."

"Yes, I know, but the entire force broke the law with this harebrained scheme to arrest innocent people. The CPS won't wear it. A prosecution would be political dynamite. I'm here to discuss your compensation claim. Now, when you see Dr Toogood, be sure to ask for a report on your physical and mental state, and whether or not he considers it arose as a result of the trauma of detention."

"But won't I be going to prison? How do you know the CPS won't be going ahead, matter of principle and all that?"

"Shouldn't tell you this, but let's put it this way. If, hypothetically, a criminal KC had a mutual back-scratching hotline to the CPS big shots and he was informed, unequivocally, that a given case was going nowhere, well, you get the idea?"

"How much will you be charging?"

"I'm doing this pro bono. My payment is in the satisfaction of playing some part in preventing manifest injustice. Everything goes around...someone will help me one day."

Rodney had just finished the paintwork on his hobby model Viking ship when Josh appeared with Jenny, in their jimjams.

"Dad, that's amazing, it's brilliant."

"No, you can't make that, Dad, it promotes violence."

"Rubbish, Jenny. Dad, can I take it to school?"

"That's not fair. I want one."

"You said it promotes violence, Jenny."

"I've changed my mind, Josh. Actually, Dad, could you make me a battleship, like the Bismarck in World War 2?"

"How did you know about that? I thought all war books had been modified so as not to cause stress and offence."

"Sorry, we bought some from Blackboys Old Bookshop with our pocket money...brilliant stuff!"

Rodney got to work.

Chapter 12.

THE MINISTRY OF ABRIDGED EDUCATION

The Ministers and their top civil servants were in a closed meeting. Philippa Featherbrain was in the chair, flanked by Mavis Netwetter and Donald Duckster. Philippa opened.

"It's appalling. I'm shocked and appalled. How dare these Headmasters breach their remit. We'll have to sack the lot. Yes, Donald?"

"Bit hasty, sorry, but all the teachers will strike and all the parents will start marching through the streets again, with placards accusing us of wanting an Orwellian culture."

Mavis took up the theme.

"There are also considerable problems at the Ministry of Rewrites. Many of the staff have left on principle and the ones remaining are finding the load impossible."

Philippa scowled. "Why, Mavis?"

"Take for example the Bible. We have to remove any form of sexism, racism, violence, frightening episodes, well, that doesn't leave much. The Old Testament is pretty much a write-off but the New is not much better. Turning water into wine has to go, promotes drinking. Raising the dead has to go, can't mention death. Throwing out the money changers involves violence, like the Good Samaritan. I think we're keeping some of the Sermon on the Mount and the feeding of the 5,000, but that's about it! Then there's other religions, but they all have similar problems. In literature generally, almost all poetry is about love, war or death, so even where we keep it it needs trigger warnings on every line and the whole meaning is basically lost. I believe 'Twinkle, twinkle little star' is still okay. Greek and Roman mythology has stirred people's creativity for centuries, but now it all has to be banned, as sexist, racist, violent and immoral.

Revising the OED is a nightmare. There are so many words in English, and so many have multiple or ambiguous meanings, there's hardly a word in it that can't cause offence or distress to someone, particularly someone who wants to be offended! As for history, don't go there. It won't be history by the time we have written most of it out, but even that is a tall order. There's a row on about the Holocaust: if we leave it in it causes fear and distress, and makes anyone of German ancestry feel bad, but if we take it out that makes the relatives of the victims feel offended and their relatives' sufferings marginalised. And they worry that it becomes more likely to happen again."

Philippa interjected, "Well what are we supposed to do?"

"Excuse me Minister, Roland Briggs here. I have a very simple solution. Why don't we revert to being the Department of Education and refuse the government directive to change everything, rather like those headteachers and the police subordinates?"

Applause throughout the meeting and motion carried.

The proceedings were leaked and the Home Office followed suit. There would be no prosecution of Geraldine, and Harriet was reinstated in the new Department of Education.

The Government then faced a vote of no confidence.

Chapter 13.

SUCCESS

Jenny and Josh were back at school, surrounded in the playground.

"Josh, please can I have a look, that ship's amazing and the characters look real. Do the rudder and tiller work?"

"Of course, Baxter, it all works. It's a replica of an old Viking ship and its crew."

Jenny's friends threw down their plastic Barbies and Jane, the Head Girl, was first in line.

"What is it, Jen?"

"It's a model of the Bismarck, a German battleship sunk by the Royal Navy in World War 2."

"That's so cool, and brilliantly scary, is it all true? Where did you get it? Can we get that stuff?"

Minis Bjorg pushed through. "I want one, it's miles better than stupid pink Barbie and her crap wardrobe."

"Yeah, and that narcissist Ken with his man boobs."

"Language, Ola", Jane in Head Girl mode.

The Headmaster was summoned to observe the commotion and then found himself giving the kids impromptu lessons on Viking history and World War 2.

Eventually, Rodney found himself inundated with orders from parents, specifying all number of unique handcrafted models. But it was the headmaster's call that made him determined to reopen his business.

"Hello, Headmaster Granger here. How are you? I have approached the Department of Education about funding for your craft models as educational aids. I've never seen the kids so engrossed, needing feeding mentally, awakening their creativity and so forth. I'd like to place a large order. But please fulfil mine first; other Heads will be getting on the bandwagon soon."

Rodney needed help, and quickly. He placed an advertisement for skilled craftspeople. This time, he worded it carefully, he would not be scuppered this time:

'Wanted, skilled City and Guilds craftspeople, to start immediately. This work is sub-contracting only. The successful Applicants will be wholly and exclusively responsible for their own workload, taxation, holiday and sickness arrangements and so forth. The sub-contracts will be for an initial period of 6 months, renewable thereafter according to workloads. For further information please contact...'

"Gerry, you're going to have to look after the children now, you're the only one not back at work."

"Sorry, Rodders, they've not just reinstated me, I've been commended and promoted for my courage in speaking out. We'll have to get a paid nanny."

"Not Nanny Bligh. Her compensation claim may have failed but it caused us so much stress and worry. We'll have to advertise."

Chapter 14.

THE NANNY

"Gerry, I've sifted through piles of applicants, chased up references. This is the one that stands out, Gunnhilda."

"Let me see her paperwork Rodders. Oh, Norland Nanny, worked for the Fothergill-Frogston-Armitages for some years, seems to have spent a few years in Helsinki with the Grange-Guthertons, outstanding references. Oh, there's more. She's clearly not work-shy and her remuneration is remarkably reasonable given her provenance. Yes, I'll sort an interview."

Jenny and Josh felt they were far too old for a nanny.

"We don't need one, it's embarrassing" they chorused. "We're not being collected or taken to school by a nanny, no way."

"Josh, I take you, your friends' parents take them, what's the problem?"

"That's different." Jenny was cross.

Sensing a rather tense atmosphere, though not understanding the words, Phoebe started screaming. You could just about hear the knock at the door.

As soon as Gunnhilda entered time just stood still. She was almost mesmerising. A head of long golden hair, tied neatly in a bun, high cheekbones, barely-there makeup, starched clean white shirt and navy skirt, not too sensible heels and long white gloves. Her voice was resonant. Reading Rodney's thoughts from his drooling body language Geraldine gave him a sharp and well-deserved 'nudge'.

"Jenny, Josh, a little gift, and here, my beautiful one, Phoebe."

Phoebe reached out for cuddles with Gunnhilda, while she engaged Jenny and Josh with amazing stories about Nordic mythology. They really were spellbound.

"Still have a problem with being ferried around by a nanny?"

"No" they said in unison, "Shush Mum, don't interrupt Gunnhilda."

It was some time before Geraldine could prise them away for the interview, although in fairness both Rodney and Geraldine, having witnessed her amazing interaction with the children, felt it was a done deal.

Eventually it was agreed that she would start the next day.

"Oh, nearly forgot, Gunnhilda."

"Yes, Mr Bottomley?"

"Oh, call me Rodney, please."

Geraldine squirmed.

"Before you leave, please can you just fill in a few details on this form. I'll have to sort out your tax and national insurance as you will formally be an employee, albeit a very treasured member of the family."

Geraldine had never seen Rodney behave in such an ingratiating and cringe-worthy fashion. She wondered if he was going to offer to lick her boots, well Louboutins anyway. There was something about Gunnhilda that she found most unsettling. Similar to the feeling she had had about Marian. No, she dismissed it as jealousy, because there was a considerable amount of that.

"All done, Rodney, here's your form. I must fly…yes, fly."

"Gerry"

"What is it, Rodders? You've got your nanny, she's done the form, I want a drink."

"It's a bit odd, she's made a mistake about her date of birth."

"For heaven's sake, Rodders, give it here."

Geraldine read the form:

'Name: Gunnhilda Lokisdottir

Born: 1st January 2000 BCE.

It happened again. Time stopped. The spell was broken by Jenny rushing

in.

"Mum, that gift from Gunnhilda…it's two packs of cards, but they've got 8

jokers!"

Printed in Great Britain
by Amazon

28922569R00066